Old LAUNCESTON

by

John Neale

In treasured memory of
Marjorie Longman of North Petherwin who taught me to read, write and to love books,
and of Bert and Margery Tremain who first opened my eyes to the history around me in Launceston.

Launceston's square in the early twentieth century, photographed on market day. Agricultural implements are on show as traders try to tempt local farmers into buying the latest piece of machinery. The ladies have put on their Sunday best to come to town.

ACKNOWLEDGEMENTS

I would like to offer my sincere thanks to the following people, without whose unstinting help this small volume would never have seen the light of day. Lloyd Goodman; Colin Barrett; Charlie and Gloria Cottle; Arthur Wills, town archivist, for reading the manuscript and giving generously of advice, comments and suggestions; Joan Rendell; Gerald and Audrey Fry; Wilfred and Marion Cocks; Peggy Tozer; Sid Broad; Douglas Lewis; Jim Edwards; Leslie Baker; John Gillbard; John Ellacott; Vera Ellacott; Bill Roberts; Austen and Winnie Robbins; Michael and Brenda Hatch; Howard and 'Josie' Ward; Ron Haste; the late Mr C. Rattray; Reg Hicks; staff at the Launceston branch of the Cornwall County Library (who always found time to help me locate obscure pieces of information despite the difficult times facing them), particularly Miss Clare Stanbury and Mrs Joy Hancock; Terry Knight and staff of the Local Studies Library at Redruth; Tony Bawden of Southgate Studio, Launceston. Lastly but by no means least, I would like to thank those whom I have quizzed about 'Old Launceston'. If I have inadvertently failed to mention anyone then I hope they will accept my deepest apologies.

Right: Looking back towards the town from a point on St Stephens Hill just below St Joseph's Dominican Convent. The trio of landmarks make this skyline as familiar to Launcestonians as that of Manhattan is to New Yorkers. From left to right they are the tower of St Mary Magdalene Parish Church; 'Big Wesley', the Central Methodist Church (whose spire was taken down in 1984); and the castle.

FURTHER READING

The books listed below were used by the author during his research. None of them are available from Stenlake Publishing. Those interested in finding out more are advised to contact their local bookshop or reference library.

Ching, John, *Reminiscences of Launceston*, Brimmell Brothers, 1907.
Cocks, Wilfred, *Launceston Methodists 1884–1984*.
Devon and Cornwall Record Society and P. L. Hull, *Cartulary of Launceston Priory*, 1987.
Rendell, Joan, *Gateway to Cornwall*, Bossiney Books, 1981.
Rendell, Joan, *Launceston: Some Pages in History*, Landfall Books, 1993.
Rendell, Joan, *Around Launceston*, Chalford, 1997.
Toy, Spencer, *The Parish Church of St Mary Magdalene, Launceston*, Parochial Church Council, 1963.
Toy, Spencer, *The Methodist Church at Launceston*, Trustees of the Wesley Methodist Church, Launceston, 1964.
Toy, Spencer, *Launceston Savings Bank*, Trustee Savings Bank, Launceston, 1967.
Venning, Arthur, *The Book of Launceston*, Barracuda Books, 1976.
Venning, Arthur; Wills, Arthur, *Yesterday's Town: Launceston*, Barracuda Books, 1988.
Venning, Arthur; Wills, Arthur, *Launceston in Camera*, Quotes Ltd., 1991.
Old Cornwall, Journal of the Federation of Old Cornwall Societies, various issues.
The Cornish and Devon Post and Launceston Weekly News.

INTRODUCTION

Launceston, pronounced 'Lanson' by the natives, is one of Cornwall's most historic towns. It occupies high ground a short distance from where the River Tamar threads its way through lush, largely agricultural landscapes and effectively marks the border with neighbouring Devon and the rest of England. Launceston has many facets to its long, proud history. The settlement dates back to Saxon times when there was a mint, a college of secular canons and a thriving market at St Stephens. There is more than a grain of truth in the age-old rhyme 'St Stephens was a market town when Launceston was a fuzzy down'. The decline of St Stephens, however, set in after Count Robert of Mortain moved the market to Dunheved Castle.

Early in the twelfth century the Bishop of Exeter dissolved the college of secular canons, later installing Augustinian canons from London on a new site by the River Kensey in the valley at Newport. This priory eventually became one of the largest and wealthiest foundations in the West Country, and remained so until its dissolution on 24 February 1539. Afterwards stone from its buildings was carted away by the townsfolk for use elsewhere until little visible remained. When work was underway to push the London & South Western Railway line on towards Padstow, the ruins were unearthed. More were revealed when an additional gas holder was built for the Launceston Gas Company in 1929.

Despite vociferous claims from other places, Launceston is the capital of Cornwall, as borne out by a royal charter granted by Philip and Mary in 1555 and supported by other charters. The town's status has never been rescinded in favour of anywhere else, and as far as Launcestonians are concerned the argument ends there!

The Norman castle overlooking the town and surrounding countryside was built within 60 years of the Conquest by William the Conqueror, the first Earl of Cornwall, and later passed to his half brother Count Robert of Mortain. Launceston is the only walled town in the county and is proud to call itself the 'true gateway to Cornwall' after its massive South Gate, the only remaining gateway to the old town. (The west and north gates were torn down many years ago, and there was never an east gate as the land falls away steeply on that side.)

Launceston has always been staunchly royalist, its motto being *Royale et Loyale*. In 1907 an application was made to the Earl Marshal (the Duke of Norfolk) for a badge borne on a standard. This was granted later the same year and gave Launceston a singular honour, it being the first borough in England to have its own standard. This was ceremoniously unfurled

on the castle and remained in regular use until 1954 when it was laid up in St Mary Magdalene Church. It is to Launceston that HRH the Prince of Wales comes to claim his feudal dues as Duke of Cornwall.

Launceston has three ancient Anglican churches – St Stephens, St Thomas the Apostle, and St Mary Magdalene – along with the Central Methodist Church, a Salvation Army citadel and a Roman Catholic church dedicated to St Cuthbert Mayne, a priest who after his arrest near Truro in 1577 was brought to Launceston, put on trial for his religious beliefs, and executed in the town square. The Quaker George Fox, founder of the Society of Friends, was imprisoned in Doomsdale, a noisome prison by the north gate of the castle. His crimes had been to distribute religious tracts at St Ives and to refuse to remove his hat to the judge when on trial at Launceston.

Situated on the upper reaches of the Tamar where the river can be more readily crossed, and between the heights of Dartmoor and Bodmin Moor, Launceston stands in a strategically important location. It played its part during the English Civil War when a skirmish took place on an area of high ground overlooking the town, known as Windmill today. Fortunately the town walls and castle were found to be impregnable and Launceston was never captured – only slighted.

As Launceston grew in wealth and importance fine Georgian town houses were built in Castle Street and elsewhere. During the Napoleonic Wars, Launceston was a parole town and French prisoners, most of them officers, were billeted with well-to-do families who lived in and around Castle Street.

The Launceston Turnpike Trust was formed in 1760 and was responsible for several nearby parishes as well as the town itself. It was disbanded in 1879. Toll-houses at St Stephens, Town Mills, Dutson and No. 34 Westgate Street remain, while the one at Pages Cross (once known as Carolina Cottage) and another at Pennygillam have been demolished.

Prior to the Parliamentary Reform Act of 1832, Launceston regularly returned four MPs to Parliament. At one time the county assizes were held in the town. They were moved to Bodmin in 1838 and the Crown court sits in Truro today.

The nineteenth century saw something of a building boom, with Launceston expanding beyond its old town walls. Municipal buildings were erected, the Launceston Savings Bank was opened, and the Public Assistance Institution at Pages Cross was built. In 1862 the Launceston Hospital and Rowe Dispensary was established in Western Road. Several large chapels, built by a variety of nonconformist groups, punctuated the streetscape. Industry began to develop with tanning, milling, and iron-founding concerns growing up near the River Kensey at Newport. For over 200 years a serge factory operated on a site now given over to the Newport Rest Garden. Public houses were plentiful, and by the middle of the nineteenth century Launceston boasted over 40. The Jubilee Inn closed in December 1909, while the Turks Head, London Inn and many others have long since gone. The Association Chapel in St Thomas Road, dating from 1840, closed in 1946. It became a brush factory the following year and was torn down in January 1998. Only the minister's residence (built in 1876) remains.

The most dramatic happening in nineteenth century Launceston was the arrival of the Launceston & South Devon Railway in 1865, later incorporated into the Great Western Railway . The London & South Western Railway, which subsequently became the Southern Railway, reached Launceston in 1886. Opinion was fiercely divided as to the advantages or otherwise of the railways. Supporters believed that they would halt the population decline and improve the town, while another faction was less enthusiastic.

During the First World War the town hall was used as an auxiliary hospital, and graves in the churchyard of St Thomas form a poignant reminder of that time. In 1921 the Butter Market in the town square was torn down and the war memorial took its place. The outbreak of the Second World War saw an influx of British service personnel to the district. Later, American servicemen came to Launceston. There were two camps, one at Pennygillam and another at Hurdon, housing black and white personnel respectively. In September 1943 tension due to the segregation and a change to the alternating weekly black/white dance rota led to what has since become known as the Battle of Launceston. Shots were fired in the square and Westgate Street, causing personal injury and bullet damage to shop windows and buildings. Bullet marks could still be seen until relatively recently. A number of soldiers were arrested and court-martialled, but the findings of the hearings were never made public, although legend has it that at least one soldier was hanged. Older Launcestonians still recall the crowds of bewildered evacuee children arriving at the station from their city homes. Others remember the bombs that were dropped at Park Lanson Farm.

The speed of change in Launceston quickened after the Second World War. One casualty was Madford House, which was demolished to make way for the Crown Offices (opened in 1964). Northgate Street and Tower Street, areas of close-knit communities, quaint buildings, courtyards and alleys, were cleared for modern housing. In 1965 Launceston lost both its railway lines and an industrial estate now covers the site of the former stations. Other vanished landmarks include the Hender Memorial, which has gone from Guildhall Square; St Mary's Hospital at Pages Cross; several tannery buildings at Newport; Tower Street Chapel; the Tower Cinema; the arched entrance to Coronation Park and the old cattle, poultry and sheep markets. The former site of the sheep market is now occupied by a multi-storey car park. Westgate Street's famous horse chestnut tree was felled on Sunday 1 September 1991.

Some buildings have survived by being converted to other uses. Pendruccumbe, originally a private girls' school, is now a nursing home. The former Horwell Grammar School for girls in Dunheved Road is the registry office and magistrates courts. Miller House nursing home stands on the site of the school's tennis courts. The National School in St Thomas Road has become the Enterprise Tamar Centre. Shops too have changed, with the likes of Folley's delicatessen; Barriball & Sons, grocers; Treleaven's ladies' and gents' outfitters; Nuttall's menswear and Gillbard's ironmongers all remembered with affection. In September 2000 F. T. Martin's electrical shop in Westgate Street ceased trading after many years, followed by Curry's in January 2001, after 52 years' trading in the High Street. The last vestiges of J. B. Smith's garage, office and workshops in Western Road were demolished in December 2000.

Launceston still continues to grow, and at the time of writing there are three housing estates being developed: Castle View in St Stephen's Hill, Kensey Parc at Eastfield, and a third development at Wooda. Plans for a fourth in the River Kensey valley are being strongly opposed.

I hope that this book will be of interest to those who know something of Launceston, and will encourage others to search out more of the Launceston of yesterday. Those who love the town and its unique history carry a responsibility to safeguard and record this history, and pass it on to future generations. Today is tomorrow's historical yesterday, and in the spirit of the Old Cornwall Movement we must 'Gather up the fragments that remain, lest they be lost'.

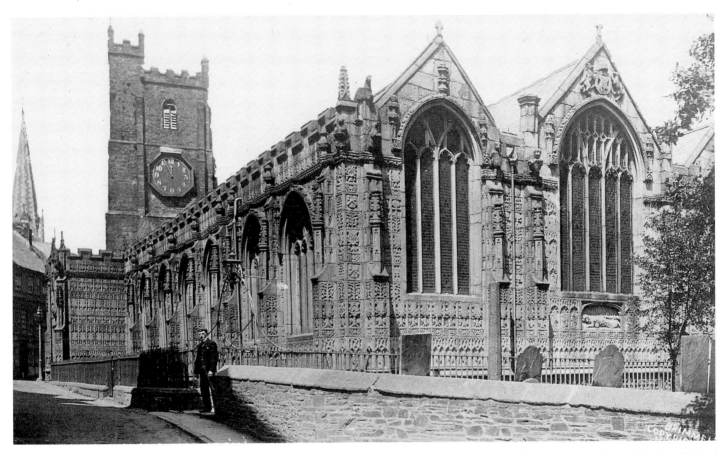

Small cottages used to stand between St Mary Magdalene Parish Church and its thirteenth century tower, but these were demolished in 1851 when the Duke of Northumberland built a council chamber on the site. This remained in use until 1881 when the present Guildhall was built. The old chamber was then acquired by the church as a choir vestry. The present St Mary's was built by Henry Trecarrell following a family tragedy. Legend has it that in 1511 Trecarrell's infant son was being bathed by his nurse and was drowned. At the time Trecarrell was building a large country mansion at Lezant. He abandoned building work and immediately had the stone carted to Launceston where St Mary Magdalene's was built over a period of 13 years. The clock that was originally installed in the tower in 1433 is reputed to have been the first public clock in Cornwall. The present clock dates from 1824. On the exterior, below one of the eastern windows, lies the recumbent figure of St Mary Magdalene. Tradition has it that if a penny (or more frequently today, a small pebble) is tossed from the footpath and lodges on the figure a new suit of clothes will be forthcoming and any reasonable wish made will almost certainly be granted.

At one time the Upper Market House – more popularly known as the Butter Market – dominated the town square. It was built in the nineteenth century after the town fathers decided that holding markets selling literally everything in the streets – including cattle – was hazardous to traders and buyers alike. A Plymouth architect, George Wightwick, who had designed several buildings of a similar type in Cornwall, was approached on the matter. He proposed having two buildings – an upper and a lower market house. The scheme was accepted and the necessary steps were taken to proceed. In its heyday the Butter Market was the focal point on market days, with all kinds of locally-grown produce brought from the surrounding districts to be sold by

farmers and their wives. This situation continued until the early 1920s when proposals were put forward to demolish the building to make way for the war memorial. There was an outcry, and a rash of correspondence flooded into the editorial office of the local newspaper, *The Cornish and Devon Post and Launceston Weekly News*, some from writers living well outside the paper's general circulation area. From whatever side of the fence it came, every letter was equally passionate. Vivian Lobb of Kelmscott Manor, at Lechlade in Gloucestershire, for instance, wrote that 'the square should be open for all to see, not filled with useless masonry'. Local man Mr Baron Lethbridge of Tregeare took the view that the Butter Market should be kept. A Mr Wenmoth living nearby said that it was a nuisance. He was fed up with the noise day and night, observed that it would take a lot of money to repair, and said that in his view the building was a waste of space and stone. As a prime site for development it should go, he said. This picture shows demolition in progress in 1921, and 80 years on it is a matter for conjecture whether Mr Wenmoth's forthright opinion had anything to do with the eventual outcome. The clock which surmounted the Butter Market is thought to have come from nearby Hexworthy House and is probably one of the last remnants of the old market building. Today it can be seen above the entrance to the town hall.

6

A red-letter day in Launceston in May 1921 as HRH Edward Prince of Wales lays the foundation stone of the war memorial. The stone was held in position by a tripod and chain and when the Prince released it, it fell smoothly into place. Ex-servicemen and the disabled had to apply for seats in the enclosure at 9/6*d*. each, while there was no charge for standing room. To gain a better vantage point some people climbed on to the remaining walls of the Butter Market. Others watched from the windows of Giddins & Williams and the Star Supply Stores. The Prince came to Launceston from Cotehele House by way of Western Road, and left via Tavistock Road – people living along the route were asked to decorate their houses. There were no decorations at the memorial site, however, in keeping with the solemnity of the occasion. When the completed memorial was unveiled the following October, the mayor commented during his speech that of Launceston's population of around 4,000 souls, 700 had served in the navy or army during the war.

The square around 1928, showing the war memorial, which was erected by a Mr Bolt. Its architect, Mr Stallybrass, was somewhat unhappy with the overall workmanship at the time of its completion. Apparently pieces of masonry had fallen off the memorial, and he instigated urgent repairs before he would agree to officially hand the structure over. Arbitration stated that Mr Bolt had to undertake certain repairs himself or get someone else to do the work at his expense. All seems to have been made good, as the memorial is still standing. On the right in the foreground is Fitze and Sons hardware shop. The business was subsequently taken over by Timothy White's and Taylors.

Being in the middle of a largely agricultural area, field sports are important to the people of Launceston. Fox hunting has always been popular, and a Boxing Day hunt assembling in the square was a long-standing tradition. This S. S. Gimblett picture shows the East Cornwall Hunt on a snowy morning in the early 1920s without a protester in sight. Dunn's grocery delivery van is also in the picture.

Passions always run high during the run-up to parliamentary elections in North Cornwall; being a marginal constituency, it is always fiercely contested. In March 1979 the Conservatives were determined to oust the sitting member and fielded their biggest gun during the election campaign. When Margaret Thatcher came to Launceston she visited the Abru Aluminium ladder factory on the Pennygillam industrial estate. The factory (which ceased production in 1997) originated in a small hut and grew to employ 70 people at its peak, exporting ladders to sixteen countries. Mrs Thatcher met members of the workforce, and tried her hand at working some of the complex machinery used in the ladder-making process. This picture shows her in the square being presented with a 'real' Cornish pasty by Peter Smale, a baker in the Parsons brothers' Duchy Bakeries. Looking on is Gerry Neale, prospective Conservative candidate for North Cornwall, and a somewhat bemused Mrs Lorna Pawling, nursing sister at Launceston General Hospital.

For many years Treleaven's was 'the' fashionable shop in town. This picture shows the main windows in Southgate Street just prior to the closure of the business in the 1970s. The premises are now occupied by the Halifax Building Society.

Ruth Sleeman outside her florist's shop at the junction of Southgate Place and Angel Hill. The business closed on Mrs Sleeman's retirement in the mid-1980s. The Southgate Wool Shop, next door, closed in 1988. Both premises have been through several transformations since and at the time of writing are being used by a shoe repair and high quality leather goods shop.

Southgate Street in the early twentieth century. On the left is Treleaven's ladies' and gents' outfitters with Proctor and Kents ironmongery and hardware shop beyond. The Georgian building beyond that was the birthplace in 1758 of Philip Gidley King, one of Launceston's celebrated sons. He joined the navy in 1770 as a midshipman, and later founded a convict settlement on Norfolk Island. Eventually he became the third governor of Tasmania at a salary of £1,000 a year – as a result the city of Launceston, Tasmania is named after this small Cornish town The Kings Arms Hotel (the Bakers Arms since 1989) is adjoining, and in the corner next to the arch Mr Adams used to keep his newsagents shop. The slate-hung building on the right is currently occupied by the Oxfam shop. Keen-eyed readers will notice that the doorway has been altered. The passageway known as Chings Alley is on the same side of the street. Large wine vaults were located there in the nineteenth century and these were put up for auction in March 1921. They failed to reach the reserved price of £1,150, and were later bought by a Mr Stonelake by private treaty.

The Southgate Arch formed part of the old town wall, and a small cottage previously occupied the area where the smaller pedestrian archway now stands. In the 1880s the arch was bought by Richard Peter, town clerk, who had it restored to mark Queen Victoria's Diamond Jubilee in 1897. Later it became the town museum until that was moved to the Passmore Edwards Institute building (old library) in Northgate Street. Today the museum is in Lawrence House in Castle Street. There were once several prisons in the town and the arch previously served as the debtors' prison. It was known as 'the dark house', probably with some justification. In 1952 the sycamore tree which grew out of the arch was thought to be damaging the structure, and after some controversy it was cut down in 1953 by Ted Hutchings, Harold Barber and other council workmen. It is customary for end-to-enders, those hardy souls travelling from John O' Groats to Lands End in a wide variety of ways, to be met by the mayor and town crier at the arch on arriving at Launceston. Beckerlegge's jewellers shop later moved to the High Street. Jessie Raddall formerly ran a saddlery business in the shop in the corner under the awning, and for some years afterwards the premises were used by the Southgate Photographic Studio. Barriball and Sons, one of the town's leading grocers, had a small shop in Southgate Place. Many older people will recall the area in the right foreground more familiarly as 'Hardy's Corner', named after a hairdressing business carried on there for many years.

These semi-derelict buildings on Market Street have recently been revamped. At one time Cotterell's fish and chip restaurant was located here, and afterwards Jan's second-hand furniture store. Today a high-class china and gift shop occupies part of the premises. The mural showing incidents in the town's history was painted by the Attic Art Group, comprising Kevin Wadland, Cecil Cole, Nancy Bowyer-Smith, Jenny Martindell and others. The group had a studio and gallery nearby.

The Tower Cinema, described at one time as the most up-to-date cinema in Devon or Cornwall, was built on the site of the Fire Engine House and was opened in August 1935 by the Mayor, Mr W. H. Gilbert. The first day's takings were donated to the Launceston Hospital Building Fund, which at the time was struggling to exceed £700. The first film shown was *D'ye Ken John Peel*, which had been released the previous year and starred Stanley Holloway, Winifred Shotter and Leslie Perrin. It was specially chosen as it was about fox-hunting, a popular pastime in the district, and it was thought the film would have enough appeal to fill the house. Seat prices were 1/9*d.*, 1/6*d.* and 8*d.*, with reductions for children.

In the cinema's heyday, the queues were features in themselves, stretching beyond Treleaven's Corner in one direction and to St Mary Magdalene Church in the other, particularly when a thriller such as *The Phantom Light* (another 1934 release) was on the bill. This had been filmed on location at Port Gaverne and Boscastle, fishing villages a few miles away, and the scenery was easily recognisable. During the last war it was Gracie Fields and George Formby who drew the crowds, particularly the troops.

The crunch came for the cinema in the 1980s, when attendances dropped drastically. In an effort to try and keep the Tower going it was taken over by a young, enterprising management team, but sadly screenings ceased in March 1983 with bingo sessions ending a month later. The 'For Sale' sign on the door in this photograph says it all. Shortly afterwards it was made known that the LADS (Launceston Amateur Dramatic Society) were keenly interested in buying the building for conversion into a small theatre, but the proposal never came to fruition and the Tower, beloved by so many in the early years, was later demolished. A modern block of flats called Market Court now stand in its place.

The Tower is also visible in the picture opposite. The building to its left was the Lower Market House, once a centre for the meat trade, with steep steps leading down to the fish market. During the Second World War, as recalled by Charlie Cottle, it was used as an air raid shelter, having had a wall of sandbags built around it. Pupils from the National School used to go there for instruction on fitting their gas masks. In 1963 Robert Cook and Co. moved their wool business to Hurdon Way and the ground floor of the Lower Market House became empty. Afterwards it was secured by the town council under a compulsory purchase order. Later the interior was remodelled and occupied by Colwill's furniture shop under the name the Tower Showrooms. In more recent years the old building has been turned into a shopping arcade.

HIGH STREET, LAUNCESTON.

The High Street in the 1920s. Kneebone's china shop occupied this prominent corner position until its closure in the early 1950s. One Launceston resident told me recently how as a child he remembers seeing vast quantities of china arriving at the shop in huge wicker crates packed with straw. It always amazed him how nothing seemed to get broken and how someone always managed to get all the straw back into the crates and push the lids down. Today the premises are occupied by Briggs shoe shop. The former Blakes ladies' shop next door is now home to a firm of solicitors. All the shopfronts on the left have been modernised, as has the old Castle Temperance Hotel premises. Who today remembers the popular 'How Do' Snack Bar? Thomas Hicks' house can be glimpsed on the extreme right of the picture (by this time Kneebone's had taken over the ground floor). Hicks was a sixteenth century mayor whose initials are carved in the granite window lintel of the building. This is believed to be one of the oldest continually-inhabited houses in Launceston.

16

A 1905 postcard of Westgate Street with the Butter Market just visible in the background and a carriage turning into the White Hart Hotel stables. Dingley and Pethybridge's Bank, with its elaborately carved frontage, was established in 1855. It was subsequently absorbed by the National Provincial Bank, which in turn was taken over by the National Westminster Bank. In the early 1870s Launceston had the distinction of being the only West Country town with more than three banks, putting it on a par with Exeter, Bristol and Bath. In November 1968 Raddall's, a sports and leather goods shop in Westgate Street, was gutted by fire. The intensity of the blaze badly damaged Pooley's fruiterers and confectioners and the Royal Insurance office, whose premises were either side. Fire-fighters from Liskeard and Callington were called to assist those from Launceston and battled until dawn. The blaze was eventually contained, although a large quantity of Christmas stock was lost. The Kneebone and Bate families, who occupied flats in adjoining premises, were rescued.

The Drill Hall in Westgate Street, photographed shortly after it was opened in October 1907. The hall was built after Mr J. C. Williams of Werrington Park made an interest free loan of £800 available. Work involved the removal of a group of dilapidated cottages on the site known as 'Noah's Ark', which were bought from the town council for £250. The hall's frontage is on Westgate Street and the side which extends back to the town hall adjoins the site of the old sheep market. It was built for C Company (Launceston) and 2 Voluntary Battalion DCLI (Duke of Cornwall's Light Infantry). Around the time the hall was built they ceased to be volunteers and became part of the Territorial Army. Today the Drill Hall is known as the Westgate Centre.

It cost £750 to purchase the site and construct the original Tower Street Chapel for the Bible Christians. The chapel opened in 1851, but in 1897 a new, larger chapel was built on an adjoining site, after which the original building was downgraded to a Sunday school. Having survived wholesale demolition and redevelopment in the area in the 1960s, the chapel was faced with another crisis in the 1970s when a decision had to be made whether or not its congregation should merge with Launceston's Methodist church. Protracted discussions took place over 2 years, and eventually a ballot was held. A slim majority were in favour of keeping the chapel as a separate entity within the Launceston Methodist circuit, but after much heart-searching its trustees recommended amalgamation and closure. The chapel closed in 1974 when the merger with the Methodist church, fondly known as 'Big Wesley', took place. This was then renamed the Central Methodist Church. Tower Street Chapel was demolished in 1982.

A variety of models of car on display in J. B. Smith's showroom in Western Road. At various periods the building has served as a Board school, egg-packing station and the Stove, Cane, Pine and Hardware Centre. It is currently called Kensey House and is the home of Stags' estate agents. The lower, rear part of the building has been transformed into flats. During the First World War volunteers packed bandages and made splints and crutches here.

The flats of Westgate Mews under construction in the late 1980s shortly after the demolition of Smith's garage in the Dockey. At this point vehicles could still use the old sheep market for parking, but its days were numbered. Today a multi-storey car park occupies the site.

The Launceston Town Band was formed in 1919 as the Launceston Municipal Band under the auspices of the Mayor, Mr J. Treleaven. The instruments played were cornets, clarinets, drums and tenor-horns. In the early days money was tight, and jumble sales and whist drives were held to raise the wind. Bandmaster Mr F. Wicks was paid the grand sum of £50 per year. The first batch of uniforms were provided by Treleaven's at a cost of £62 6s. 6d. in 1924, but were not paid for until 1932. In this more recent picture the band are seen marching through the square under the capable direction of bandmaster Reg Walters. Among the bandsmen pictured are Reg Gale, Ron Haste, Bill Northey, Donald and Richard Dymond and Charles Ward. The business premises are interesting too. Fitze and Son's is now occupied by Boots the Chemists, the Joy Shop is Finlay's newsagents and the Midland Bank has become HSBC.

This Walter Weighell of Launceston photograph from the early 1970s shows an Armistice Sunday parade entering the square. The parade is being led by Wing Commander Robinson and bandmaster Ben Luxton. Among those featured are Ivor Thomas, F. Worth, M. Beard, B. Worth, M. Stoneman, H. Ward, W. Frayn and Mandy Thomas. Standard bearer Bert Tremain brings up the rear of the first contingent.

Launceston Town Band in position and waiting for the call to order prior to an Armistice Sunday parade. Among those pictured are bandmaster Reg Walters, bandsmen Ron Haste, Reg Gale, Tim Symons, E. Uren, Les Olver, W. Goodman, G. Deacon, E. Couch and D. Dymond. The mysterious doorways in the wall in Western Road were built up with concrete blocks by English Heritage workmen in March 1993, causing a hue and cry. Later they were faced with natural stone. The first doorway to be so blocked was the one at the end of Castle Dyke.

In 1897 the Launceston Liberal Association's new headquarters in Northgate Street were completed. They were built on the site of some run-down cottages and boasted a red-brick and tile-hung frontage with projecting corner oriel windows and square bays under a gabled roof. There were spacious reading and games rooms on the upper floors, as well as smoking and non-smoking rooms, as some members objected to having to mix with those who smoked. In that respect the club was years ahead of its time! The headquarters were officially opened in June 1898, when their exterior was lavishly decorated with ivy and evergreens interspersed with cream, white and pink roses. Flags were strategically placed among the foliage. Older Launcestonians will remember Hilda May, who took up the tenancy of the shop underneath the club in 1958 selling high-class ladies fashions. In 1978 the building to the right, adjoining the club, came up for sale and was subsequently secured by the Liberal Association for £11,500. It opened in 1981. The fourteenth century Bell Inn, one of the oldest public houses in town, can just be glimpsed in the background.

NORTHGATE STREET, LAUNCESTON.

The top end of Northgate Street looking towards St Mary Magdalene Church and the Liberal Club. Most of the buildings in the foreground of this view were demolished in 1964 to make way for modern housing as part of a three-year development programme. Few people in the immediate area welcomed the scheme, which effectively destroyed one of the oldest parts of Launceston. George Oke and George Brendon, who both lived in Northgate Street, had very strong opinions and one local shop keeper, Mr Rowe, said the redevelopment was 'a disgrace'. Several families were moved to other parts of the town; most were concerned about the additional rent they would have to pay on moving to modern estates elsewhere in the town.

Having crossed the River Tamar at Polson Bridge, visitors approaching Launceston from the Okehampton direction soon reach Kensey View, which looked like this in 1914. The picture is almost certainly posed and was taken by Fred Mitchell, who advertised himself as 'Tourist Photographer, Launceston'. These houses enjoy a beautiful view over the wide expanse of the River Kensey valley. One wonders, over 80 years later, what the people pictured would have thought about the current plan to build in the valley, a move which is being vigorously opposed. During the summer months, holiday traffic used to grind up this hill nose to tail, often having to halt at the bottom in order to allow those at the top to negotiate the hairpin bend by Prouts garage, whose business closed in January 1992.

Until the bypass between Lifton Down and Tresmarrow was opened on the southern side of the town in 1976, streams of holiday traffic crawled along Tavistock Road day and night, making life a nightmare for residents, particularly at weekends. It was part of the old A30 trunk road, and lengthy traffic hold-ups and overheated car engines were the order of the day. The bypass, built by McAlpine & Son (Southern Ltd), cost over £5 million and took less than 2 years to complete. Among the first to drive along the new route were the Mayor and Mayoress, Mr and Mrs Wilfred Bailey. People who feared that the new road would kill the town have been proved wrong. The vast number of juggernaughts which hurtle down the main route miss the town, while private motorists still visit in large numbers – and there is still congestion.

In July 1931 a grand pageant, depicting events from the town's history between 1089 and 1862, fired the imagination of Launcestonians. Written by Miss Mary Kelly, it was produced by a Mrs Evans, assisted by a nucleus of sub-producers. The pageant was performed on the Castle Green and over 400 people took part. Apparently the main problems encountered were casting the chief roles in each scene and the inclement weather, which drastically curtailed rehearsal time. Everyone threw themselves into the production with enthusiasm, and the costumes, scenery and horse-trappings were made voluntarily to keep expenses down. This scene features part of episode five, concerning the arrival of the Great Western Railway in Launceston. The part of Mr Richard Robbins, one of those far-sighted townsmen who could see all the benefits of the railway and fought vigorously for it against strong opposition, was played by Mr W. H. Bickley. A note on the back of this picture states that all the ladies wore crinolines and the men sported top hats and frock coats. Music during the performance was provided on a public address system supplied by Messrs Wroe and Briggs of Bude. The event was hailed as a roaring success and the proceeds from the occasion went to several health-related organisations.

This was one of the non-agricultural attractions at the Launceston Horse Show at Pennygillam in 1920, the second such show following the break caused by the First World War. On this occasion the weather was 'catchy': slight showers overnight prevented local farmers from carrying on with the hay harvest, but meant that many took the opportunity to visit the show. Almost all classes were filled to capacity, and there were 140 horses, 60 cattle and 50 pigs on show, as well as a wide range of dairy products. Lunches were provided by Mr E. Reed, one of Launceston's leading bakers and confectioners. As this picture shows, musical entertainment during the day came from the band of HMS *Renown*. In the evening they gave a public concert on the Castle Green. Launceston Town Band, which was then in its infancy, played until 10 p.m.

Launceston Mayor, Councillor Jim Hughes, was a highly-respected Welshman who hailed from Aberdare, Glamorgan. It was army service that brought him to Cornwall, and Launceston in particular, where he was in charge of German and Italian prisoners of war at nearby Werrington Park. He joined the town council in 1957, holding his seat for 37 years. This photograph from July 1987 shows him setting off from outside the White Hart Hotel in grand style, complete with familiar bowler hat, to visit the Launceston Centenary Agricultural Show, still known as the Horse Show among the farming community. The four greys and stagecoach are the pride and joy of Mr William Tucker. Despite the rain the coach and its occupants arrived at the showground to a rapturous welcome from the 6,000-strong crowd. 'Taffy' Hughes, the little Welshman with the big heart who was mayor of Launceston three times, died in July 1996.

St Thomas Hill, popularly known as Old Hill, in the early twentieth century, showing the view northwards towards St Stephens and the countryside beyond. The children's clothing reflects the styles of the time. One Launceston lady whose family home was in Old Hill remembers as a small child how after a snowfall they used metal or wooden trays to sledge down the hill, only to crash headlong into the railway bridge at the bottom. This would be even more hazardous today because in recent years sleeping policemen have been installed on the hill as a traffic-calming measure. Who today remembers buying sweets from Mrs Tink's shop near the top of the hill or Penno's (now the launderette) further down?

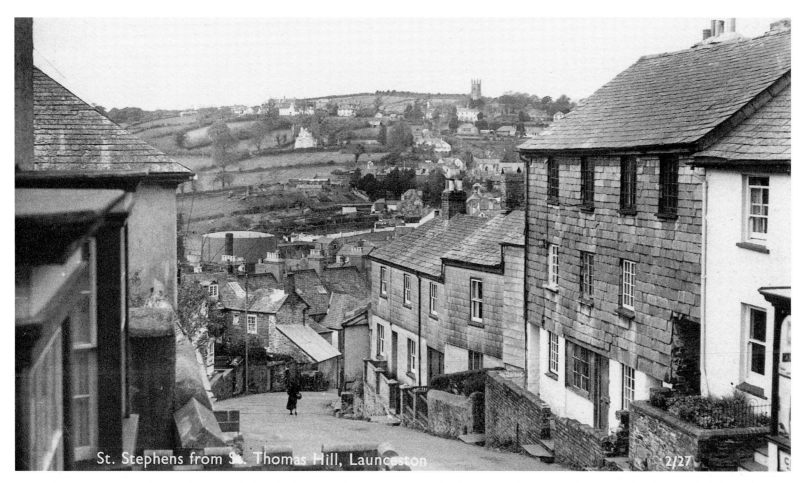

St. Stephens from St. Thomas Hill, Launceston 2/27

When the go-ahead was given to build a third gas holder, seen in the middle of this picture of St Thomas Hill, the town's other two holders were only just managing to cope with demand. The new gas holder was built by Willey Co. Ltd. of Exeter and was inaugurated in December 1929 by Dr W. F. Thompson, director of the Launceston Gas Company, having taken only nine months to build. At the time its statistics must have been mind-boggling. It was 62 feet in diameter, rested on a reinforced concrete base 21 feet deep, and was made of steel plates held together with 82,000 rivets. The gas holder was removed in 1990, and housing developments now cover the fields in the middle of the picture. A new development, Castle View, is currently being built. The keen-eyed will notice that St Joseph's Dominican Convent school extension does not appear in the picture. This dates from 1960 and increased the school's boarding facilities as well as providing additional classrooms.

The Launceston Public Assistance Institution was opened in 1837 and the first master of the new workhouse was a Mr Gruzelier. Many casuals (tramps) came for a night's lodging, a bath, food and occasionally a change of clothing. They were expected to chop firewood and break stones for road repairs. Fruit and vegetables were grown in the workhouse's extensive gardens, and at one point over 8 tons of potatoes were lifted and stored at Pages Cross. In December 1948 it was thought wise to investigate the possibility of purchasing a light cultivator. Models were subsequently demonstrated by Watkins and Roseveare and the Launceston Farm Implement Company, and the committee bought a 'Trusty' tractor shortly afterwards. This picture shows part of the old frontage at Pages Cross Workhouse sand-bagged during the Second World War. The couple are believed to be Mr and Mrs Leonard Horwell of Newton Abbot. The main entrance was demolished in the 1960s.

In 1948, with the advent of the National Health Service, the Launceston Public Assistance Institution was renamed Pages Cross Infirmary and became St Mary's Hospital the following year. St Mary's specialised in the care of the elderly and had its own day unit and occupational and physiotherapy facilities. At one time in the 1960s there were almost 100 patients and nearly as many nursing and ancillary staff, all of whom were under the care and direction of the last matron, Miss G. H. King, until her retirement. Afterwards the hospital was run by sisters-in-charge, nursing officers, and hospital managers.

Christmas was always a special time for patients and staff at St Mary's Hospital. In the build-up to the great day the wards were lavishly decorated, groups of carol singers visited, and occasional nativity plays were performed by Sunday school groups. On Christmas Eve the staff and their friends held a candlelit carol service. On Christmas Day itself, staff on some of the wards wore fancy dress on a given theme which was different each year. Those that spring to mind are circus-time, pantomime characters and John O' Groats to Lands End, where one end of the ward had a Scottish theme and the other end was Cornish. In the kitchen Christmas cakes, Christmas puddings and mince pies were made by the score, as well as a whole range of other seasonal fare. Nothing mass-produced was bought in. In this picture, taken on Christmas Day 1959, Reg Baker, one of the male nursing staff, is showing his expertise (probably to the chagrin of the cooks) in carving one of several turkeys. From left to right, the other three in kitchen uniforms are Sylvia Cann, Dawn Chubb and Marjorie Lane. Casting an eye over the proceedings from the head of the table is Mrs Betty Sluggett.

The closure of St Mary's Hospital was announced in November 1988, but it struggled on until the end of March 1992 when the few remaining patients were transferred elsewhere. Shortly afterwards the building was boarded up. The final indignity came in 1994 when the demolition squad moved in and the complex was razed to the ground. The site has since been extensively redeveloped by Tesco.

Alan John Vidler (Joe to everyone in Launceston), who died in 1989, was a popular character in and around the town. He came to Launceston from Tunbridge Wells, married and settled, and for a number of years ran a furniture removal and storage business based in St Thomas Road until ill-health curtailed his driving and forced him to retire. He was a regular member of St Mary Magdalene Church choir and a part-time fireman. He is pictured here with his equipage, including his pony Trixie, who he bought for £100, thereby saving her from certain slaughter. Joe and his turnout was a star attraction at the Launceston Agricultural Show and also at the vintage steam rally at Polson where he enjoyed giving pony rides to children and visitors alike. The photograph was taken at the junction of Dunheved Road and the part of Westgate Street still known as Police Station Hill. The building behind Joe is the old county police station of 1885, which is now in private ownership. The names of the small apartments echo its former use.

Launceston fire brigade carrying out one of their more pleasant duties – raising the bunting in the square (Dunn's Corner) to celebrate the Queen's Silver Jubilee in 1977. Lennard's shoe shop, formerly the Public Benefit Boot Company, closed in September 1988 following a company merger which resulted in the loss of five jobs locally. Mrs Betty Davey was manageress at the time. The premises are now occupied by the Alliance and Leicester Building Society. Davey's, on the opposite corner, is now home to Philip Warren and Son, butchers.

One of the worst fires Launceston experienced in several years occurred in February 1992 at Spry's Garage in Exeter Street. The car showroom, built in the 1930s, was gutted and over 40 vehicles were destroyed. At the height of the inferno the Launceston fire brigade were assisted by brigades from Callington, Liskeard and Tavistock, with over 50 firefighters actively engaged in tackling the blaze at one point, directed by Divisional Fire Officer Graham Collins and Station Officer Norman Furse. A vast quantity of water was used, drawn from hydrants at Prout's Corner, Madford Lane, Race Hill and from the reservoir under the square. The gentleman in the foreground is Brian Worth.

The heat from the blaze was so intense that the frontage of the garage workshops on the opposite side of the street was badly scorched. The landlord of the Launceston Arms public house was awakened by stones being thrown against the windows, and residents in No. 6, across the road from the pub, had to be rescued by firemen using breathing apparatus. Several dogs were also saved. This photograph of the aftermath shows the devastation in Exeter Street. Spry's subsequently moved to the Pennygillam industrial estate where they took over the old Smith's garage building.

New Road, or more correctly St Thomas Road, with a horse-drawn cart in the distance. In 1910 heated discussions took place in the council chamber regarding the cost of a granite footpath from the National School to Mr Hawkins Corner. Apparently two people tendered for the job, a Mr Nankivell of Bodmin and a Mr Tinney of Launceston. It seems that Mr Nankivell's tender was 14 shillings cheaper than Mr Tinney's, but he would only have the granite brought to the railway station, while Mr Tinney would deliver it to the site! It was felt that Mr Tinney ought to be supported as he was a local man, although alderman Treleaven asked why the council were prepared to throw away 14 shillings. Some of the buildings on the right in this picture have been demolished to make way for modern development, while Vosper's, the newsagents on the left, closed its doors long ago. A heavy volume of traffic continually uses St Thomas Road now, particularly during the Launceston rush hour.

This photograph of the National School in St Thomas Road was taken soon after its closure in the early 1970s when it was feared that the building was sliding down the hill and might collapse at any moment. The school was built in 1840 at a cost of £495. One former pupil, the late Alf Perkin, told me that when he started school there the first two words he learnt to spell were 'Wooda' and 'Tredydan', road names which are both still prominently displayed on the wall of the school and that of a nearby house respectively, and that is how he found his way home. Several old scholars were involved in the school's restoration, and today the exterior looks very much as it always did. Inside it has been remodelled and is now home to a number of small businesses in its new role as the Enterprise Tamar Centre.

This picture of Newport Square was taken in 1911; the calf standing in the cart at the bottom of St Stephens Hill suggests it was market day. The Round House was built in 1829 by the Duke of Northumberland and was officially called the Temple of the Winds. Today it protects the old market cross, and is known colloquially as Newport Town Hall, because the results of elections were formerly announced from it. At one time it was pressed into service by Mr George Burt as a builder's store. He bequeathed it to Launceston Town Council. In 1992 the building was given a much-needed facelift when wrought iron window grills and iron gates were installed and it was painted. The shop on the extreme right of the picture was once W. T. Doidge's ironmongers, and was then taken over for a short period by Marshall Vanstone. It became S. C. Bickle's in 1950, but they sold the business in 1965 and relocated to the town centre in 1968. Flooding was once a regular curse at Newport, sometimes occurring four or five times a year. On one occasion in 1960 local firemen worked for 23 hours non-stop when the River Kensey swamped houses in Westbridge Road. At the height of the flood these were under 4 feet of water. In the 1980s a flood prevention scheme was put in place and residents in Westbridge Road now have little fear of serious flooding.

Probably no part of Launceston has seen more change than Newport. If only this old picture looking from the White Horse public house towards the town could speak. The houses in the left foreground have been demolished (the firm of Hillman's plumbers was based there until the 1980s), and Greenaway's garage premises now occupy most of this area. The tannery building beyond the river bridge with its distinctive gable end and louvred upper storey (see page 44) has also been levelled. On the right the bulwark of Holne House stands defiant, while the two gas street lamps have been replaced. Part of the area behind the wall between them used to be the Cornwall County Council depot. Today it is a used car parking lot for the garage opposite. The entrance to the Newport industrial estate now stands in the middle of the scene, along with Launceston's first set of traffic lights, which came into use in November 1991.

When King Edward VII died in May 1910 Launceston was plunged into deep mourning. Flags flew at half-mast and inside the council chamber the silver maces were draped in black. Well-attended memorial services were held in all the main churches. This picture shows the solemn proclamation of the accession of King George V at Newport, one of five locations where the ceremony takes place, the others being outside the Guildhall, at the Southgate Arch, at Northgate (the old library) and on St Stephen's Green. As always, the ceremony was attended by large crowds of interested onlookers. Who was the small boy who found a handy vantage point on top of the London & South Western Railway parcels delivery van? It is on record that when the ceremony was being enacted outside the Guildhall, Launceston's centenarian Mr Richard Peter, accompanied by his grandson, was present and joined in lustily. On that day Mr Peter had lived in the reigns of six monarchs.

At one time Newport Square was a popular place for the Stowford Beagles to meet. This picture from the 1970s shows them with (left to right) Reg Hicks, whipper-in for twelve seasons, Des Walker and hunt master Philip Mayne. They usually met at Newport four times a year. Glimpsed behind the car is Horwell Villa, once a boys' grammar school.

Launceston, St. Thomas's Church.

Picturesque St Thomas the Apostle Church at Riverside viewed from the St Thomas Road river bridge. The louvred building was part of Reed's tannery concern and later served as Moore's builders store. It was demolished in the 1970s to make way for St Thomas's church hall. The weir too has been removed and the river generally cleaned up to ease water flow and help flood prevention.

Every community was touched by the Great War in one way or another. Countless servicemen died far from home. One was a Scotsman whom Launcestonians took very much to their hearts. He was Sergeant Whyte of the 1st Battalion Gordon Highlanders, one of six sons of Mr and Mrs John Whyte of Glasgow, four of whom were in the army. This picture shows his military funeral in St Thomas's churchyard in April 1916. Sergeant Whyte was 20 years old and died of septicaemia at the auxiliary hospital. He had been severely wounded at Loos, was moved back to the army base camp hospital in France, then moved again to the VAD Hospital at Newton Abbot. He finally came to Launceston to convalesce. While Sergeant Whyte's parents and two brothers were in Launceston for the funeral they received the news that another son had been killed. The cortege left the auxiliary hospital with the coffin draped in the Union flag. Sergeant Whyte was buried next to a comrade, Private Harding, of the 6th Worcesters. At the end of the service a volley was fired over the grave by a party sent through from VAD headquarters at Exeter.

This is all that remains of the Augustinian Priory which was founded here in 1126. At the time of its dissolution in 1539, it was one of the largest and richest such foundations in the country. Through subsequent centuries Launceston people filched stone for building to such an extent that nothing visible remained. Traces of the priory were only discovered centuries later when excavations were in hand to push the London & South Western Railway line deeper into north Cornwall. No one knows exactly how extensive the priory grounds were, but it is believed that they stretched to where the modern-day St Thomas Road passes the Railway Inn – and possibly as far as Wooda and the old National School. Some historians say that Priory Park was built on the priory herb gardens. In 1976 a service (pictured above) was held amid the ruins after the site had been cleaned up by members of St Thomas Youth Club. A new initiative, the Launceston Priory Project, is now dedicated to preserving the ruins.

Fronting the street on the town side of the St Thomas Road river bridge, this building was part of the Hender tannery complex. It was partly demolished in August 1984 and levelled the following Christmas. Greenaways Garage can be glimpsed on the opposite side of the river.

This photograph shows one of the last surviving tannery buildings in Launceston. The mill race and waterwheel were taken away in the early 1980s when the River Kensey was widened.

For a small Cornish town, Launceston was uniquely well served by railways, boasting two stations side by side. The Launceston & South Devon line (later owned by the Great Western Railway) came up from Plymouth and the London & South Western, later the Southern Railway, arrived in the town from Exeter and Okehampton. For most of the time they shared a signal box. Among the Southern Railway station staff pictured here just prior to the Second World War are: H. Godbeer, signalman; Harry Bishop and Fred Wright, porters; Walter Greenslade, stationmaster; the manager of the W. H. Smith bookstall, Mr Passmore; Jim Walters, district inspector; Mr Palk, cattle inspector; and the station dog, Tiny, a great favourite with station staff and passengers alike.

This picture shows what was almost the last market day at Race Hill in 1991. Prior to the market being opened in January 1900, cattle and other animals had been sold in the square. The excavations that were undertaken on the sloping site – which was something in the order of 3 acres in extent – were remarkable. The market was on three levels, each one several feet above the other, with the main entrances on Race Hill. Access was also provided from the Exeter road, opposite Cook's stores, giving an easier route to and from the railway stations. 91 years after it opened, protracted talks were held concerning several alternative out-of-town market sites, with locations at Kennard's House, Lawhitton, and Trebursye being considered. None of these options came to fruition, and in the event the cattle market closed seemingly overnight and moved to Hallworthy, some miles away. Launceston's days as a true market town had ended, though older generations still come into town on Tuesday – 'market day'.

Soon after J. B. Smith's garage in the Dockey ceased trading, the premises were bought by a large supermarket chain which acquired No. 2 The Dockey, an eighteenth century listed building in the conservation area, shortly afterwards. The cottage had once been part of the Westgate Inn complex with stabling for several horses at the rear. Proposals for its demolition were later floated. Local people and traders went up in arms, and over 1,000 signed a petition in an effort to try and persuade planners to reprieve the cottage. Despite the petition and protests from individuals, as well as the Launceston Old Cornwall Society, it was demolished in 1985. The proposed supermarket failed to materialise as a preservation order was placed on part of the old town wall at the rear of the site. The last occupants of the cottage were Mr and Mrs Victor Lake. Today part of Westgate Mews stands on its site.

Since this picture of the Coronation Park was taken in the 1950s, all the buildings have been demolished to make way for a modern leisure centre. The land, a triangular field of around 8 acres immediately adjoining Windmill, was given to the town by Mr C. H. Gillbard in 1937. The gift was also endowed by £5,000. The main entrance to the park faced Dunheved Road, with concrete piers supporting two fancy carriage gates and a white concrete bridge between the piers carrying the name of the park in green lettering. Unfortunately the imposing entrance was swept away in recent years to allow lorries access during the latest upgrading of the amenities.